The Choice Is Yours

-

I'm Not Just A Pretty F.A.C.E, I AM Intelligent Too

Yasmine Ben Salmi aka Lovepreneur

Yasmine Ben Salmi aka Lovepreneur

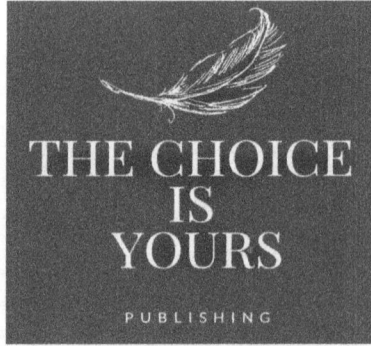

THE CHOICE
IS
YOURS

PUBLISHING

The Choice Is Yours

DEDICATION

This book it dedicated to all girls and women around the world that are strong, kind, adventurous, smart, intelligent and most importantly unique.

FOREWORD

"Don't Act Like A Girl", "Girls Are Weak", "Women Can't Be Scientists!", "Women Shouldn't Have An Opinion", "You're Not Pretty Enough", "It happened Because Of What She Was Wearing", "That Goes Against The Dress Code, It's Distracting"

For the longest time women and young girls have been devalued, disrespected, oversexualised and dehumanised by society and the media…

In this phenomenal book by the Award-Winning Author Yasmine Ben Salmi, you will be taken on a journey of empowerment and re-education around the topics of sexualisation, education and so much more as she redefines what it means to be a WOMAN.

Now more than ever young women (and women as a whole) need to be supported and guided to enable them to step into their full potential and embrace their uniqueness. For the first time in history, we are now in a position to redefine what it means to be "girl" or "women", we are powerful, we are strong, we are INTELLIGENT, we are wise, we are creative and we deserve to be heard, seen, respected and celebrated!

As you go through this process of growth, re-education and exploration, I want you to commit to paying the knowledge and growth forward. You can do this by sharing this book with someone that you know, be that a young girl, or a friend of your mother.

I feel so honoured to know Yasmine and to have her as my sister because at the mere age of 11 years old she made it her mission to teach young women how to reclaim their power and to step into their fullest potential whilst embracing their beautiful and powerful femininity.

Always remember that you are beautiful, perfect and unique just the way you are so don't let anyone tell you otherwise!

- Lashai Ben Salmi

ACKNOWLEDGMENTS

Just before I start this book, I would like to take a moment to acknowledge all the amazing and intelligent and caring women in my life.

CONTENTS

INTRODUCTION

Hi, my name is Yasmine Ben Salmi, and I am 14 years old. I wrote this book because I wanted to inspire you to start discussions about the way society sexualises and objectifies women and girls. As a result, society has created beauty standards and a host of expectations that girls and women feel pressurised to follow. Nowadays, there is the added factor of social media, and this has pushed this matter to the forefront of triggering anxiety, depression and so much more because of all the unconventional pressures that girls and women face upon a daily basis. It really saddens me when I hear men or boys downgrade women and also go as far as rating women bodies. It is my aim to help put an end to these awful and heart-breaking habits.

My dream is to become a plastic surgeon and to open my own international clinic that aims to help people who have experienced tragic accidents. I'm really looking forward to helping as many people as possible to acknowledge that beauty is on the inside and not what society deems it to be.

I want the world to know that behind every pretty F.A.C.E we women and girls, are more than just facial features and body figures that people just look at and admire, we should be known for our intelligence, our drive to learn, and our natural ability to love everything that comes our way.

INTELLIGENT

Let's first talk about how intelligent we are as women and how much we have to offer to this world, for example Harriet Tubman who led more than 300 enslaved people to freedom, she also helped to ensure an end to slavery in the United States by Aiding the Union during the American Civil War. Harriet Tubman also worked as a scout and a nurse, despite receiving little pay or recognition, for her work. Reading about Harriet made me realise that we as women can make a difference, and I'm not saying for you to go out and end a war, but I am saying that we as women, as girls and as females should use our intelligence to make a difference and to love who we are unconditionally. When I think about the future, a world where women are not objectified and most importantly treated with respect. This vision of our future gives me so much hope for what our generation might become.

MY DREAMS

We all have dreams, and I believe that if you take action to achieve your deepest dreams it will become a reality.

I have so many dreams, and my dreams excite me. Everything begins in the heart and very great achievement began in the mind of one person. The ones who dare to dream and believe in the so called impossible until that moment when it becomes possible.

Give yourself permission to "Wouldn't it be nice if...?" more often.

My purpose is to help 1M girls and women to increase self-love by eradicating low self-esteem, my other dreams include, becoming a plastic surgeon and to one day open my own clinic, and in doing so, I need to have a lot of knowledge about it too, for that I have a lot of belief in myself.

ALLOW ME TO SHARE SOME WOMEN WHO INSPIRED ME TO WRITE:

I'm Not Just A Pretty F.A.C.E, I AM Intelligent Too

OPRAH WINFREY

Oprah Winfrey is a talk show host, media executive, actress and billionaire philanthropist. Oprah Winfrey is known for being the host of her very own TV programme called The Oprah Winfrey Show which started in 1986 to 2011 with 25 seasons. Then in 2011 she launched her TV network called, OWN. Oprah Winfrey didn't always have an easy life as when she was a teenager she became a mother at the age of 14 after being molested, during her childhood and as an early teen, not only that her son who was born prematurely died in infancy, shortly after she was sent to live with a man she calls her father by the name of (Vernon Winfrey) who was a barber in Nashville, Tennessee, while she was still in high school she landed a job as a radio show host, by 19 she managed to become a co-anchor for the local evening news. She then went on the inspire millions and to become this amazing woman we all see today!

Oprah Winfrey taught me that no matter how many struggles we as women, as people may face on our journey, it's important to keep going.

"The biggest adventure you can ever take is to live the life of your dreams."
-   Oprah Winfrey

MARIE KONDO

Marie Kondo is best known for her popular Netflix series called Tidying Up With Marie Kondo where she helped people to tidy up their homes and space so that they do not feel overwhelmed, and to let go of items or belongings that they no longer needed, or if the item did not serve any good for them anymore. When Marie was a kid, she always loved to tidy up, she even stated that while the other kids would go out to play for break time, she was inside the classroom tidying up the bookshelves and organising the class. So, at an early age she had a love for tidying up, and after seeing the impact that decluttering had on her she decided to share her knowledge with other people, so that they will see the results she got, and for that many people have followed the KonMari method. As a result of all the people she has helped, after her first Netflix series she has recently released a new Netflix series called Sparking Joy With Marie Kondo, where she helps people to realise whether or not their belongings spark enough joy for them, and if not then the item doesn't serve them anymore.

The KonMari method taught me the importance of tidying up, and the effects it can have on my life.

"Keep only those things that speak to your heart. Then take the plunge and discard all the rest. By doing this, you can reset your life and embark on a new lifestyle."
-   Marie Kondo

VALERIE THOMAS

Valerie Thomas is known for being the first black woman to ever build a 3D image for TV and movies, many were surprised that they had never heard of Valerie Thomas, she also claimed pioneered 3D television and movies. She is also credited with developing the illusion transmitter, the first device that used concave mirrors and light rays to generate the illusion of a three-dimensional image. Then in 1980 she was granted a patent for this invention. Her idea creates an optical illusion of a 3D image that appears real, her technology is still used by NASA today. As a child Valerie was interested in science after watching her father tinkering with the television and seeing the mechanical parts inside the TV, which she then became more curious. When she was 8, she read The Boys First Book on Electronics, which piqued her interest in pursuing a scientific career. Despite her father's interest in electronics, her father refused to assist her with the projects in the book. She was not encouraged to pursue scientific and mathematic classes at the all-girls school she attended, however she did manage to take a physics course. In the early years of the Landsat programme, she was in charge designing the digital media formats image processing systems.

Valerie Thomas taught me that even without support from people we love the most, never ever give up.

"Hobbies are for wimps who don't have the guts to follow their passion"
- Valerie Thomas

MALALA YOUSAFZAI

Malala Yousafzai is best known as a child activist who campaigned against the Tehrik-i-limitations Taliban's on girls' education. Malala Yousafzai was a young girl in Pakistan when she stood up to the Taliban and demanded that girls be allowed to attend school. She was shot three times in the head by a Taliban gunman in 2012, yet she miraculously survived. She received the Nobel Peace Prize in 2014, making her the youngest person in history to do so. Malala goes across the world inspiring young girls to be role models and to lead by example, as Malala does. Malala proves that she is unstoppable in a variety of ways. As a result of her involvement in such activities, she is able to educate others. Malala Yousafzai is also known as a young activist; Malala displays that she indeed unstoppable in several ways. She can educate others as a result of her participation in such activities she has had the chance to meet inspirational people just like her such as, Greta Thunberg who is a young Climate change activist, she has also met some amazing other women in power like, Michelle Obama, and Emma Watson, and many more. She has recently been given the chance to become the face of British Vogue which was amazing to see.

Malala taught me that, in the world everyone has their own purpose, and everyone was put on this earth to make a positive difference.

"Education is education. We should learn everything and then choose which path to follow. Education is neither Eastern nor Western, it is human."
- Malala Yousafzai

HARRIET TUBMAN

Harriet Tubman was born a slave in the Maryland county of Dorchester around the year 1820. She started working as a house servant when she was about five or six years old. She was sent to labour in the fields seven years later. She sustained an injury when still in her early teens that would affect her for the rest of her life. Harriet suffered a terrible brain injury when she was thirteen years old. It happened while she was in town on a visit. When a slave owner attempted to throw an iron weight at one of his slaves, it instead struck Harriet. She nearly died as a result of the injuries, which left her with dizzy episodes and blackouts for the rest of her life. Harriet had a very unimaginable start to life, also being 5 years old and whipped when your slave owners baby cried. Harriet Tubman was so determined, she made sure she saw an end to the slavery in United States, and how she helped lead over 700 enslaved people to freedom. Tubman's pseudonym was "Moses," and she spent her entire life illiterate. She was afflicted with narcolepsy. Her work as "Moses" was extremely important to her. She never had a slave go missing. During the Civil War, Tubman served as a Union scout. She was able to treat dysentery. She was the first female combat commander.

Harriet Tubman taught me that no matter what struggles may come your way, you will always surpass them and bring people along to become stronger, and to fight for what is right.

"Every great dream begins with a dreamer. Always remember, you have within you the strength, the patience, and the passion to reach for the stars to change the world."
- Harriet Tubman

RUTH BADER

Ruth Bader was a lawyer and jurist who served in association justice of the Supreme Court of the United States from 1993 until her death in September 2020, which was very devastating for many people who know her personally and for those who thought of her as an inspiration to dream big and to achieve whatever it is, that they want to become in the future. One of her biggest achievements in my opinion was when she got nominated by President Bill Clinton, replacing retiring justice Byron White. She also spent most of her legal career as an advocate for gender equality and to help fight for women's right, in doing so she won many arguments before the supreme court. In the 1970s, she worked as a volunteer attorney for the American Civil Liberties Union, serving on its board of directors and as one of its general counsels. In the 1970s, she worked as a volunteer attorney for the American Civil Liberties Union, serving on its board of directors and as one of its general counsels. Her story continues to inspire many people around the world to achieve their very best. Despite two bouts with cancer and public requests from liberal legal professors, she refused to step down in 2013 or 2014, when Democrats could pick her replacement.

Ruth Bader taught me that no matter what challenges you may face in life, medical and spiritually never give up!

"Women's rights are an essential part of the overall human rights agenda, trained on the equal dignity and ability to live in freedom all people should enjoy."
-    Ruth Bader

MISTY COPELAND

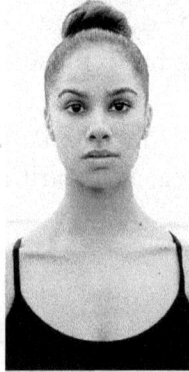

Misty Copeland is an American Ballet dancer from America Ballet Theatre, which is known as one of the three leading classical ballet companies in the United States. Then on June 30, in 2015, Copeland became the first African American woman to be promoted to principal dancer in American Ballet Theatre's 75- year history. Misty was in love with ballet since the age of 13 years old, she was also considered a prodigy who rose to stardom despite not starting ballet at her early age. Two years later, in 1998, Misty's ballet teachers, who were serving as her custodial guardians, and her mother, fought custody over her, even while Misty was already an award– winning dancer and was also fielding professional offers. She was born in Kansas City, Missouri and was raised in San Pedro, California, Misty began her Ballet studies at the age of 13 years old at the San Pedro City Ballet. Then later at the age of 15 she won 1st place in the Music Centre Spotlight Awards. She began her studies later at the Lauridsen. Ballet Centre. American ballet dancer who, in 2015, became the American Ballet Theatre's first African

American female principal dancer (ABT), she became a member of ABT's Studio Company in 2000 and its corps de ballet in 2001, and became an ABT soloist in 2007.she has been recognised by many inspirational people around the world such as Obama and his two daughters by the names of Malia Anne Obama and Sasha Obama, she has met many more inspirational people along her journey.

Misty Copeland taught me that age is just a number, and if you put your mind to it, you can do achieve.

"I may not be there yet, but I am closer than I was yesterday"
- Misty Copeland

MOTHER TERESA

Mother Teresa is mostly known for being a famous Catholic Nun who dedicated her life to caring for the destitute and dying in the slums of Calcutta – which is also now known as Kolkata. During the time Mother Teresa was alive she won the Nobel peace prize in 1971 due to her acts of kindness and being a humanitarian and an advocate for the poor and helpless. Besides for her passion for helping serve the poor, she changed the world by inspiring people what universal love means, having universal love in helping people doing the smallest things, one act of kindness. Universal love became one of the core principle of the Missionaries of Charity, which is the organization she founded that now have millions of members all over the world. In contrast to her setting up Missionaries of Charity she also quoted that they "lived like animals but die like angels." Mother Teresa grew up in the Roman Catholic Church and decided to devote her life to holy work also referenced as "Godly Work" and this was decided at an early age, later when she turned 18, she joined the Sisters of Loreto in order to become a missionary to India. But before she could go to India, she had to learn English, in order to learn she spent a year in Ireland practicing and learning to speak English at the Loreto Abby.

Mother Teresa taught me that no matter how much money I have or make, always devote it to help others who might not have the same privilege as you.

"There are no great things, only small things with great love. Happy are those."
- Mother Theresa

KARREN BRADY

Karren Brady was born in Edmonton, London, her family's house was situated near the Tottenham Hotspur football ground. When Karren was a teenager, she was academic as she attended Salcombe Preparatory school which was later followed by A boarding school by the name of Poles Convent located in Ware, Hertfordshire, after she finished both primary school and secondary school, she attended an all-boys school by the name of Aldenham School, Elstree, as the school accepted girls in the sixth form. Later in Karren's life she began as a trainee at an advertising company called Saatchi & Saatchi, as she was rejected for a place on a journalism course at Harlow College. Even though she got rejected She got interviewed in 2018 making a conscious decision not to go to university, she was keen on making her mark in the world. Later in 2010 she was appointed Vice-Chairman of West Ham United which was a very big achievement for her.

She appeared as a celebrity contestant on Comic Relief Does The Apprentice and team leader for girls' team which helped to raise more than £750,000. She is currently married to her husband Paul Peschisolido an Canadian footballer who played for Birmingham City for 2 seasons. She currently has 2 children by the names of Sophia and her son Paolo. She was awarded an honorary doctorate from the University of Birmingham in 2010, in the same year she was also listed in the business category of the Sunday Telegraph's 100 most Powerful Women in Britain.

Karren taught me that there are no boundaries in life and learning to inspire people from all around the world.

"Hard work will always bring opportunities."
-   Karren Brady

SYSTEM

F.A.C.E

Please allow me to take a moment to introduce you to my four-step system designed to inspire you to share your dreams with the world. It is time to share your intelligence and teach the world that you have so much more to offer because you are not just a pretty face.

F: Focus
A: Attitude
C: Connections
E: End Step

Focus – You Become What You Affirm™
I want you to take a moment to take 3 deep breaths. Then I would like you to close your eyes and focus on your desired outcome, then begin to inhale to the count of 4 seconds, hold your breath for 4 seconds and then slowly exhale to the count of 4 seconds. How would it feel inside if you were living your dream lifestyle now? Who are you that is just waiting to come out and share with the world? What brings you joy? What do you enjoy doing?

Steps:

1) List of 10 affirmations
2) Write your vision for the next 5 years and then another 5 years from that vision
3) Select an accountability partner

Attitude – Your Attitude Determines Your Altitude™
I truly believe that the best starting point is gratitude.

Steps:

4) List 10 things that you are grateful for
5) Make a list of people in your network and the potential support they could give you

6) Write a list of how you can be of service toother can you be of service to others
7) What do you need in order to feel fully supported?

Connections – **Plant 3 Seed for A Brighter Tomorrow™**
I want you to take a moment to reflect on your End Step vision. How different will the world look when you have given birth to your vision? What problems will you solve?

Steps:

8) What does connection to self me to you?
9) What does connection to others mean to you?
10) What does connection to mother earth mean to you?

End Step – **Plant 3 Seed for A Brighter Tomorrow™**
I want you to take a moment to reflect on your End Step vision. How different will the world look when you have given birth to your vision? What problems will you solve?

Steps:

11) Find a problem
12) Come up with solutions for that problem
13) Package your ideas in the form of products and services

CONCLUSION

CONCLUSION

I hope that you feel inspired after reading:

'The Choice Is Yours - I'm Not Just A Pretty F.A.C.E, I AM Intelligent Too'

In conclusion women have so much to contribute and to make our precious world a better place. Without the bold, brave, kind, noble, historical, mathematical, spiritual, humble, meek, scientific, courageous and loving contributions that women have consistently made since the beginning of time our world have been a less flavoursome reality – wouldn't you agree?...

Therefore, I encourage to take flight and pursue your deepest desires after all you are not just a pretty F.A.C.E, because you are intelligent too.

DAILY MANIFESTING
JOURNAL

DAILY MANIFESTING JOURNAL

Writing things down is an effective way of remembering and reflecting on all the amazing things that happen every day.

No matter how much you write or how little you write take the time to really think about your day, at the end of your journal you can then go back and treasure those memories.

Date: __/__/____ Today I am Grateful For...

_____

_____

_____

What Would Make Today A Great Day?

_____

_____

_____

During the evening just before going to bed take a moment to reflect on your day then List the 3 best things that happened...

1) _____

_____

_____

2) _____

_____

_____

3) _____

_____

_____

Date: __/__/____ Today I am Grateful For...

_____

_____

_____

What Would Make Today A Great Day?

_____

_____

_____

During the evening just before going to bed take a moment
to reflect on your day then List the 3 best things that
happened...

1) _____

_____

_____

2) _____

_____

_____

3)   _____

_____

_____

Date: __/__/____ Today I am Grateful For...

_____

_____

_____

What Would Make Today A Great Day?

_____

_____

_____

During the evening just before going to bed take a moment to reflect on your day then List the 3 best things that happened...

1)   _____

_____

_____

2)   _____

_____

_____

3)   _____

_____

_____

Date: __/__/____ Today I am Grateful For...

_____

_____

_____

What Would Make Today A Great Day?

_____

_____

_____

During the evening just before going to bed take a moment to reflect on your day then List the 3 best things that happened...

1)   _____

_____

_____

2)   _____

_____

_____

3) _____

_____

_____

Date: __/__/____ Today I am Grateful For...

_____

_____

_____

What Would Make Today A Great Day?

_____

_____

_____

During the evening just before going to bed take a moment
to reflect on your day then List the 3 best things that
happened...

1) _____

_____

_____

2) _____

_____

_____

3) _____

_____

_____

Date: __/__/____ Today I am Grateful For…

_____

_____

_____

What Would Make Today A Great Day?

_____

_____

_____

During the evening just before going to bed take a moment
to reflect on your day then List the 3 best things that
happened…

1) _____

_____

2) _____
   _____
   _____
   _____

3) _____
   _____
   _____

Date: __/__/____ Today I am Grateful For...

_____

_____

_____

What Would Make Today A Great Day?

_____

_____

_____

During the evening just before going to bed take a moment to reflect on your day then List the 3 best things that happened...

1) _____

_____

_____

2) _____

_____

_____

3) _____

_____

_____

Date: __/__/____ Today I am Grateful For...

_____

_____

_____

What Would Make Today A Great Day?

_____

_____

_____

During the evening just before going to bed take a moment to reflect on your day then List the 3 best things that happened...

1) _____

_____

_____

2) _____

_____

_____

3) _____

_____

_____

Date: __/__/____ Today I am Grateful For...

_____

_____

_____

What Would Make Today A Great Day?

_____

_____

_____

During the evening just before going to bed take a moment to reflect on your day then List the 3 best things that happened…

1) _____

_____

_____

2) _____

_____

_____

3) _____

_____

_____

Date: __/__/____ Today I am Grateful For…

_____

_____

_____

What Would Make Today A Great Day?

_____

_____

_____

During the evening just before going to bed take a moment
to reflect on your day then List the 3 best things that
happened…

1) _____

_____

_____

2) _____

_____

_____

3) _____

_____

_____

Date: __/__/____ Today I am Grateful For…

_____

_____

_____

What Would Make Today A Great Day?

_____

_____

During the evening just before going to bed take a moment to reflect on your day then List the 3 best things that happened…

1) _____

   _____

   _____

2) _____

   _____

   _____

3) _____

   _____

   _____

Date: __/__/____ Today I am Grateful For…

_____

_____

_____

What Would Make Today A Great Day?

_____

_____

_____

During the evening just before going to bed take a moment
to reflect on your day then List the 3 best things that
happened…

1) _____

_____

_____

2) _____

_____

_____

3) _____

_____

_____

Date: __/__/____ Today I am Grateful For…

_____

_____

_____

What Would Make Today A Great Day?

_____

_____

_____

During the evening just before going to bed take a moment
to reflect on your day then List the 3 best things that
happened...

1) _____

_____

_____

2) _____

_____

_____

3) _____

_____

_____

Date: __/__/____ Today I am Grateful For...

_____

_____

_____

What Would Make Today A Great Day?

_____

_____

_____

During the evening just before going to bed take a moment
to reflect on your day then List the 3 best things that
happened...

1) _____

_____

_____

2) _____

_____

_____

3) _____

_____

_____

Date: __/__/____ Today I am Grateful For...

_____

_____

_____

What Would Make Today A Great Day?

_____

_____

_____

During the evening just before going to bed take a moment
to reflect on your day then List the 3 best things that
happened...

1) _____

_____

_____

2) _____

_____

_____

3) _____

_____

_____

Date: __/__/____ Today I am Grateful For...

_____

_____

_____

What Would Make Today A Great Day?

_____

_____

_____

During the evening just before going to bed take a moment to reflect on your day then List the 3 best things that happened...

1) _____

_____

_____

2) _____

_____

_____

3) _____

_____

_____

Date: __/__/____ Today I am Grateful For...

_____

_____

_____

What Would Make Today A Great Day?

_____

_____

_____

During the evening just before going to bed take a moment to reflect on your day then List the 3 best things that happened...

1) _____

_____

_____

2) _____

_____

_____

3) _____

_____

_____

Date: __/__/____ Today I am Grateful For...

_____

_____

_____

What Would Make Today A Great Day?

_____

_____

_____

During the evening just before going to bed take a moment to reflect on your day then List the 3 best things that happened...

1) _____

_____

_____

2) _____

_____

_____

3) _____

_____

_____

Date: __/__/____ Today I am Grateful For...

_____

_____

_____

What Would Make Today A Great Day?

_____

_____

_____

During the evening just before going to bed take a moment
to reflect on your day then List the 3 best things that
happened...

1) _____

_____

_____

2) _____

_____

_____

3) _____

_____

_____

Date: __/__/____ Today I am Grateful For...

_____

_____

_____

What Would Make Today A Great Day?

_____

_____

_____

During the evening just before going to bed take a moment to reflect on your day then List the 3 best things that happened...

1) _____

_____

_____

2) _____

_____

_____

3) _____

_____

_____

Date: __/__/____ Today I am Grateful For...

_____

_____

_____

What Would Make Today A Great Day?

_____

_____

_____

During the evening just before going to bed take a moment
to reflect on your day then List the 3 best things that
happened...

1) _____

_____

_____

2) _____

_____

_____

3) _____

_____

_____

Date: __/__/____ Today I am Grateful For…

_____

_____

_____

What Would Make Today A Great Day?

_____

_____

_____

During the evening just before going to bed take a moment to reflect on your day then List the 3 best things that happened…

1) _____

_____

_____

2) _____

_____

_____

3) _____

_____

_____

Date: __/__/____ Today I am Grateful For...

_____

_____

_____

What Would Make Today A Great Day?

_____

_____

_____

During the evening just before going to bed take a moment
to reflect on your day then List the 3 best things that
happened...

1) _____

_____

_____

2) _____

_____

_____

3) _____

_____

_____

Date: __/__/____ Today I am Grateful For...

_____

_____

_____

What Would Make Today A Great Day?

_____

_____

_____

During the evening just before going to bed take a moment
to reflect on your day then List the 3 best things that
happened...

1) _____

_____

_____

2) _____

_____

_____

3) _____

_____

_____

Date: __/__/____ Today I am Grateful For...

_____

_____

_____

What Would Make Today A Great Day?

_____

_____

_____

During the evening just before going to bed take a moment
to reflect on your day then List the 3 best things that
happened...

1) _____

_____

_____

2) _____

_____

_____

3) _____

_____

_____

Date: __/__/____ Today I am Grateful For...

_____

_____

_____

What Would Make Today A Great Day?

_____

_____

_____

During the evening just before going to bed take a moment
to reflect on your day then List the 3 best things that
happened...

1) _____

_____

_____

2) _____

_____

_____

3) _____

_____

_____

Date: __/__/____ Today I am Grateful For…

_____

_____

_____

What Would Make Today A Great Day?

_____

_____

_____

During the evening just before going to bed take a moment to reflect on your day then List the 3 best things that happened…

1) _____

_____

_____

2) _____

_____

_____

3) _____

_____

_____

Date: __/__/____ Today I am Grateful For...

_____

_____

_____

What Would Make Today A Great Day?

_____

_____

_____

During the evening just before going to bed take a moment to reflect on your day then List the 3 best things that happened...

1) _____

_____

_____

2) _____

_____

_____

3) _____

_____

_____

Date: __/__/____ Today I am Grateful For...

_____

_____

_____

What Would Make Today A Great Day?

_____

_____

_____

During the evening just before going to bed take a moment to reflect on your day then List the 3 best things that happened...

1) _____

_____

_____

2) _____

_____

_____

3) _____

_____

_____

Date: __/__/____ Today I am Grateful For...

_____

_____

_____

What Would Make Today A Great Day?

_____

_____

_____

During the evening just before going to bed take a moment to reflect on your day then List the 3 best things that happened...

1) _____

_____

_____

2) _____

_____

_____

3) _____

_____

_____

Date: __/__/____ Today I am Grateful For...

_____

_____

_____

What Would Make Today A Great Day?

_____

_____

_____

During the evening just before going to bed take a moment
to reflect on your day then List the 3 best things that
happened...

1) _____

_____

_____

2) _____

_____

_____

3) _____

_____

_____

Date: __/__/____ Today I am Grateful For...

_____

_____

_____

What Would Make Today A Great Day?

_____

_____

_____

During the evening just before going to bed take a moment to reflect on your day then List the 3 best things that happened...

1) _____

_____

_____

2) _____

_____

_____

3) _____

_____

_____

Date: __/__/____ Today I am Grateful For...

_____

_____

_____

What Would Make Today A Great Day?

_____

_____

_____

During the evening just before going to bed take a moment
to reflect on your day then List the 3 best things that
happened...

1) _____

_____

_____

2) _____

_____

_____

3) _____

_____

_____

Date: __/__/____ Today I am Grateful For...

_____

_____

_____

What Would Make Today A Great Day?

_____

_____

_____

During the evening just before going to bed take a moment to reflect on your day then List the 3 best things that happened...

1) _____

_____

_____

2) _____

_____

_____

3) _____

_____

_____

Date: __/__/____ Today I am Grateful For...

_____

_____

_____

What Would Make Today A Great Day?

_____

_____

_____

During the evening just before going to bed take a moment to reflect on your day then List the 3 best things that happened...

1) _____

_____

_____

2) _____

_____

_____

3) _____

_____

_____

Date: __/__/____ Today I am Grateful For…

_____

_____

_____

What Would Make Today A Great Day?

_____

_____

_____

During the evening just before going to bed take a moment
to reflect on your day then List the 3 best things that
happened…

1) _____

_____

_____

2) _____

_____

_____

3) _____

_____

_____

Date: __/__/____ Today I am Grateful For...

_____

_____

_____

What Would Make Today A Great Day?

_____

_____

_____

During the evening just before going to bed take a moment
to reflect on your day then List the 3 best things that
happened...

1) _____

_____

_____

2) _____

_____

_____

3) _____

_____

_____

Date: __/__/____ Today I am Grateful For...

_____

_____

_____

What Would Make Today A Great Day?

_____

_____

_____

During the evening just before going to bed take a moment
to reflect on your day then List the 3 best things that
happened...

1) _____

_____

_____

2) _____

_____

_____

3) _____

_____

_____

Date: __/__/____ Today I am Grateful For...

_____

_____

_____

What Would Make Today A Great Day?

_____

_____

_____

During the evening just before going to bed take a moment to reflect on your day then List the 3 best things that happened...

1) _____

_____

2) _____

_____

3) _____

_____

_____

Date: __/__/_____ Today I am Grateful For…

_____

_____

_____

What Would Make Today A Great Day?

_____

_____

_____

During the evening just before going to bed take a moment
to reflect on your day then List the 3 best things that
happened…

1) _____

_____

_____

2) _____

_____

_____

3) _____

_____

_____

Date: __/__/____ Today I am Grateful For…

_____

_____

_____

What Would Make Today A Great Day?

_____

_____

_____

During the evening just before going to bed take a moment
to reflect on your day then List the 3 best things that
happened…

1) _____

_____

_____

2) _____

_____

_____

3) _____

_____

_____

Date: __/__/____ Today I am Grateful For...

_____

_____

_____

What Would Make Today A Great Day?

_____

_____

_____

During the evening just before going to bed take a moment
to reflect on your day then List the 3 best things that
happened...

1) _____

_____

_____

2) _____

_____

_____

3) _____

_____

_____

Date: __/__/____ Today I am Grateful For...

_____

_____

_____

What Would Make Today A Great Day?

_____

_____

_____

During the evening just before going to bed take a moment
to reflect on your day then List the 3 best things that
happened...

1) _____

_____

_____

2) _____

_____

_____

3) _____

_____

_____

Date: __/__/____ Today I am Grateful For...

_____

_____

_____

What Would Make Today A Great Day?

_____

_____

_____

During the evening just before going to bed take a moment to reflect on your day then List the 3 best things that happened...

1) _____

_____

_____

2) _____

_____

_____

3) _____

_____

_____

Date: __/__/____ Today I am Grateful For...

_____

_____

_____

What Would Make Today A Great Day?

_____

_____

_____

During the evening just before going to bed take a moment
to reflect on your day then List the 3 best things that
happened...

1) _____

_____

_____

2) _____

_____

_____

3) _____

_____

_____

Date: __/__/____ Today I am Grateful For...

_____

_____

_____

What Would Make Today A Great Day?

_____

_____

_____

During the evening just before going to bed take a moment
to reflect on your day then List the 3 best things that
happened...

1) _____

_____

_____

2) _____

_____

_____

3) _____

_____

_____

Date: __/__/____ Today I am Grateful For...

_____

_____

_____

What Would Make Today A Great Day?

_____

_____

_____

During the evening just before going to bed take a moment
to reflect on your day then List the 3 best things that
happened...

1) _____

_____

_____

2) _____

_____

_____

3) _____

_____

_____

Date: __/__/____ Today I am Grateful For...

_____

_____

_____

What Would Make Today A Great Day?

_____

_____

_____

During the evening just before going to bed take a moment to reflect on your day then List the 3 best things that happened...

1) _____

_____

_____

2) _____

_____

_____

3) _____

_____

_____

Date: __/__/____ Today I am Grateful For...

_____

_____

_____

What Would Make Today A Great Day?

_____

_____

_____

During the evening just before going to bed take a moment
to reflect on your day then List the 3 best things that
happened...

1) _____

_____

_____

2) _____

_____

_____

3) _____

_____

_____

Date: __/__/____ Today I am Grateful For...

_____

_____

_____

What Would Make Today A Great Day?

_____

_____

_____

During the evening just before going to bed take a moment to reflect on your day then List the 3 best things that happened...

1) _____

_____

_____

2) _____

_____

_____

3) _____

_____

_____

Date: __/__/____ Today I am Grateful For...

_____

_____

_____

What Would Make Today A Great Day?

_____

_____

_____

During the evening just before going to bed take a moment
to reflect on your day then List the 3 best things that
happened...

1) _____

_____

_____

2) _____

_____

_____

3) _____

_____

_____

Date: __/__/____ Today I am Grateful For…

_____

_____

_____

What Would Make Today A Great Day?

_____

_____

_____

During the evening just before going to bed take a moment
to reflect on your day then List the 3 best things that
happened…

1) _____

_____

_____

2) _____

_____

_____

3) _____

_____

_____

Date: __/__/____ Today I am Grateful For...

_____

_____

_____

What Would Make Today A Great Day?

_____

_____

_____

During the evening just before going to bed take a moment to reflect on your day then List the 3 best things that happened...

1) _____

_____

_____

2) _____

_____

3) _____

_____

_____

_____

Date: ___/___/_____ Today I am Grateful For...

_____

_____

_____

What Would Make Today A Great Day?

_____

_____

_____

During the evening just before going to bed take a moment
to reflect on your day then List the 3 best things that
happened...

1) _____

_____

_____

2) _____

_____

3) _____

_____

_____

Date: __/__/____ Today I am Grateful For...

_____

_____

_____

What Would Make Today A Great Day?

_____

_____

_____

During the evening just before going to bed take a moment to reflect on your day then List the 3 best things that happened...

1) _____

_____

2) _____

_____

_____

3) _____

_____

_____

Date: __/__/____ Today I am Grateful For...

_____

_____

_____

What Would Make Today A Great Day?

_____

_____

_____

During the evening just before going to bed take a moment to reflect on your day then List the 3 best things that happened...

1) _____

_____

_____

2) _____

_____

3) _____

_____

_____

Date: __/__/____ Today I am Grateful For...

_____

_____

_____

What Would Make Today A Great Day?

_____

_____

_____

During the evening just before going to bed take a moment to reflect on your day then List the 3 best things that happened...

1) _____

_____

_____

2) _____

_____

_____

3) _____

_____

_____

Date: __/__/____ Today I am Grateful For…

_____

_____

_____

What Would Make Today A Great Day?

_____

_____

_____

During the evening just before going to bed take a moment
to reflect on your day then List the 3 best things that
happened…

1) _____

_____

_____

2) _____

_____

_____

3) _____

_____

_____

Date: __/__/____ Today I am Grateful For…

_____

_____

_____

What Would Make Today A Great Day?

_____

_____

_____

During the evening just before going to bed take a moment to reflect on your day then List the 3 best things that happened…

1) _____

_____

_____

2) _____

_____

_____

3) _____

_____

_____

Date: __/__/____ Today I am Grateful For…

_____

_____

_____

What Would Make Today A Great Day?

_____

_____

_____

During the evening just before going to bed take a moment to reflect on your day then List the 3 best things that happened…

1) _____

_____

_____

2) _____

_____

_____

3) _____

_____

_____

Date: __/__/____ Today I am Grateful For...

_____

_____

_____

What Would Make Today A Great Day?

_____

_____

_____

During the evening just before going to bed take a moment to reflect on your day then List the 3 best things that happened...

1) _____

_____

_____

2) _____

_____

3) _____

_____

_____

_____

Date: __/__/____ Today I am Grateful For...

_____

_____

_____

What Would Make Today A Great Day?

_____

_____

_____

During the evening just before going to bed take a moment to reflect on your day then List the 3 best things that happened...

1) _____

_____

_____

2) _____

_____

_____

3) _____

_____

_____

Date: __/__/____ Today I am Grateful For...

_____

_____

_____

What Would Make Today A Great Day?

_____

_____

_____

During the evening just before going to bed take a moment
to reflect on your day then List the 3 best things that
happened...

1) _____

_____

_____

2) _____

_____

_____

3) _____

_____

_____

Date: __/__/____ Today I am Grateful For…

_____

_____

_____

What Would Make Today A Great Day?

_____

_____

_____

During the evening just before going to bed take a moment to reflect on your day then List the 3 best things that happened…

1) _____

_____

_____

2) _____

_____

_____

3) _____

_____

_____

Date: __/__/____ Today I am Grateful For…

_____

_____

_____

What Would Make Today A Great Day?

_____

_____

_____

During the evening just before going to bed take a moment to reflect on your day then List the 3 best things that happened…

1) _____

_____

_____

2) _____

_____

3) _____

_____

_____

Date: __/__/____ Today I am Grateful For…

What Would Make Today A Great Day?

During the evening just before going to bed take a moment to reflect on your day then List the 3 best things that happened…

1) _____

2) _____

_____

3) _____

_____

_____

Date: __/__/____ Today I am Grateful For…

_____

_____

_____

What Would Make Today A Great Day?

_____

_____

_____

During the evening just before going to bed take a moment to reflect on your day then List the 3 best things that happened…

1) _____

_____

2) _____

_____

3) _____
    _____
    _____
    _____

Date: __/__/____ Today I am Grateful For...

_____

_____

_____

What Would Make Today A Great Day?

_____

_____

_____

During the evening just before going to bed take a moment to reflect on your day then List the 3 best things that happened...

1) _____
    _____
    _____

2) _____
    _____

_____

3) _____

_____

_____

Date: __/__/____ Today I am Grateful For...

_____

_____

_____

What Would Make Today A Great Day?

_____

_____

_____

During the evening just before going to bed take a moment to reflect on your day then List the 3 best things that happened...

1) _____

_____

_____

2) _____

_____

3) _____

_____

_____

Date: __/__/____ Today I am Grateful For…

_____

_____

_____

What Would Make Today A Great Day?

_____

_____

_____

During the evening just before going to bed take a moment
to reflect on your day then List the 3 best things that
happened…

1) _____

_____

_____

2) _____

_____

3) _____

_____

_____

Date: __/__/____ Today I am Grateful For…

_____

_____

_____

What Would Make Today A Great Day?

_____

_____

_____

During the evening just before going to bed take a moment to reflect on your day then List the 3 best things that happened…

1) _____

_____

_____

2) _____

_____

3) _____

_____

_____

Date: __/__/____ Today I am Grateful For…

_____

_____

_____

What Would Make Today A Great Day?

_____

_____

_____

During the evening just before going to bed take a moment
to reflect on your day then List the 3 best things that
happened…

1) _____

_____

_____

2) _____

_____

3) _____

_____

Date: __/__/____ Today I am Grateful For...

_____

_____

_____

What Would Make Today A Great Day?

_____

_____

_____

During the evening just before going to bed take a moment to reflect on your day then List the 3 best things that happened...

1) _____

_____

_____

2) _____

_____

_____

3) _____

_____

_____

Date: __/__/____ Today I am Grateful For...

_____

_____

_____

What Would Make Today A Great Day?

_____

_____

_____

During the evening just before going to bed take a moment
to reflect on your day then List the 3 best things that
happened...

1) _____

_____

_____

2) _____

_____

_____

_____

3) _____

_____

_____

_____

Date: __/__/____ Today I am Grateful For...

_____

_____

_____

What Would Make Today A Great Day?

_____

_____

_____

During the evening just before going to bed take a moment
to reflect on your day then List the 3 best things that
happened...

1) _____

_____

_____

_____

2) _____

_____

_____

_____

3) _____

_____

_____

Date: __/__/____ Today I am Grateful For...

_____

_____

_____

What Would Make Today A Great Day?

_____

_____

_____

During the evening just before going to bed take a moment to reflect on your day then List the 3 best things that happened...

1) _____

_____

_____

2) _____

_____

_____

3) _____

_____

_____

_____

Date: __/__/____ Today I am Grateful For...

_____

_____

_____

What Would Make Today A Great Day?

_____

_____

_____

During the evening just before going to bed take a moment
to reflect on your day then List the 3 best things that
happened…

1) _____

_____

_____

2) _____

_____

_____

3) _____

_____

_____

Date: __/__/____ Today I am Grateful For…

_____

_____

_____

What Would Make Today A Great Day?

_____

_____

_____

During the evening just before going to bed take a moment to reflect on your day then List the 3 best things that happened…

1) _____

_____

_____

2) _____

_____

_____

3) _____

_____

_____

Date: __/__/____ Today I am Grateful For…

_____

_____

_____

What Would Make Today A Great Day?

_____

_____

_____

During the evening just before going to bed take a moment to reflect on your day then List the 3 best things that happened…

1) _____

_____

_____

2) _____

_____

_____

3) _____

_____

_____

Date: __/__/____ Today I am Grateful For…

_____

_____

_____

What Would Make Today A Great Day?

_____

_____

_____

During the evening just before going to bed take a moment to reflect on your day then List the 3 best things that happened...

1) _____

_____

_____

2) _____

_____

_____

3) _____

_____

_____

Date: __/__/____ Today I am Grateful For...

_____

_____

_____

What Would Make Today A Great Day?

_____

_____

_____

During the evening just before going to bed take a moment to reflect on your day then List the 3 best things that happened…

1) _____

_____

_____

2) _____

_____

_____

3) _____

_____

_____

Date: __/__/____ Today I am Grateful For…

_____

_____

_____

What Would Make Today A Great Day?

_____

_____

_____

During the evening just before going to bed take a moment to reflect on your day then List the 3 best things that happened…

1) _____

_____

_____

2) _____

_____

_____

3) _____

_____

_____

Date: __/__/____ Today I am Grateful For…

_____

_____

_____

What Would Make Today A Great Day?

_____

_____

_____

During the evening just before going to bed take a moment to reflect on your day then List the 3 best things that happened...

1) _____

_____

_____

2) _____

_____

_____

3) _____

_____

_____

Date: __/__/____ Today I am Grateful For...

_____

_____

_____

What Would Make Today A Great Day?

_____

_____

_____

During the evening just before going to bed take a moment to reflect on your day then List the 3 best things that happened...

1) _____

_____

_____

2) _____

_____

_____

3) _____

_____

_____

Date: __/__/____ Today I am Grateful For...

_____

_____

_____

What Would Make Today A Great Day?

_____

_____

_____

During the evening just before going to bed take a moment to reflect on your day then List the 3 best things that happened…

1) _____

_____

_____

2) _____

_____

_____

3) _____

_____

_____

Date: __/__/____ Today I am Grateful For…

_____

_____

_____

What Would Make Today A Great Day?

_____

_____

_____

During the evening just before going to bed take a moment
to reflect on your day then List the 3 best things that
happened...

1) _____

_____

_____

2) _____

_____

_____

3) _____

_____

_____

Date: __/__/____ Today I am Grateful For...

What Would Make Today A Great Day?

During the evening just before going to bed take a moment to reflect on your day then List the 3 best things that happened…

1) _____

_____

_____

2) _____

_____

_____

3) _____

_____

_____

Date: __/__/____ Today I am Grateful For…

What Would Make Today A Great Day?

During the evening just before going to bed take a moment to reflect on your day then List the 3 best things that happened...

1) _____

_____

_____

2) _____

_____

_____

3) _____

_____

_____

Date: __/__/____ Today I am Grateful For...

_____

_____

_____

What Would Make Today A Great Day?

_____

_____

_____

During the evening just before going to bed take a moment to reflect on your day then List the 3 best things that happened...

1) _____

_____

_____

2) _____

_____

_____

3) _____

_____

_____

Date: __/__/____ Today I am Grateful For...

_____

_____

_____

What Would Make Today A Great Day?

_____

_____

_____

During the evening just before going to bed take a moment to reflect on your day then List the 3 best things that happened...

1) _____

_____

_____

2) _____

_____

_____

3) _____

_____

_____

Date: __/__/____ Today I am Grateful For...

_____

_____

_____

What Would Make Today A Great Day?

_____

_____

_____

During the evening just before going to bed take a moment to reflect on your day then List the 3 best things that happened…

1) _____

_____

_____

2) _____

_____

_____

3) _____

_____

_____

Date: __/__/____ Today I am Grateful For…

_____

_____

_____

What Would Make Today A Great Day?

_____

_____

_____

During the evening just before going to bed take a moment to reflect on your day then List the 3 best things that happened...

1) _____

_____

_____

2) _____

_____

_____

3) _____

_____

_____

Date: __/__/____ Today I am Grateful For...

_____

_____

_____

What Would Make Today A Great Day?

_____

_____

_____

During the evening just before going to bed take a moment to reflect on your day then List the 3 best things that happened…

1) _____

_____

_____

2) _____

_____

_____

3) _____

_____

_____

Date: __/__/____ Today I am Grateful For…

_____

_____

_____

What Would Make Today A Great Day?

_____

_____

_____

During the evening just before going to bed take a moment to reflect on your day then List the 3 best things that happened…

1) _____

_____

_____

2) _____

_____

_____

3) _____

_____

_____

Date: __/__/____ Today I am Grateful For…

_____

_____

_____

What Would Make Today A Great Day?

_____

_____

_____

During the evening just before going to bed take a moment to reflect on your day then List the 3 best things that happened…

1) _____

_____

_____

2) _____

_____

_____

3) _____

_____

_____

Date: __/__/____ Today I am Grateful For…

_____

_____

_____

What Would Make Today A Great Day?

_____

_____

_____

During the evening just before going to bed take a moment to reflect on your day then List the 3 best things that happened...

1) _____

_____

_____

2) _____

_____

_____

3) _____

_____

_____

Date: __/__/____ Today I am Grateful For...

_____

_____

_____

What Would Make Today A Great Day?

_____

_____

_____

During the evening just before going to bed take a moment to reflect on your day then List the 3 best things that happened…

1) _____

_____

_____

2) _____

_____

_____

3) _____

_____

_____

Date: __/__/____ Today I am Grateful For…

_____

_____

_____

What Would Make Today A Great Day?

_____

_____

_____

During the evening just before going to bed take a moment to reflect on your day then List the 3 best things that happened...

1) _____

_____

_____

2) _____

_____

_____

3) _____

_____

_____

Date: __/__/____ Today I am Grateful For...

_____

_____

_____

What Would Make Today A Great Day?

_____

_____

_____

During the evening just before going to bed take a moment to reflect on your day then List the 3 best things that happened...

1) _____

_____

_____

2) _____

_____

_____

3) _____

_____

_____

Date: __/__/____ Today I am Grateful For...

_____

_____

_____

What Would Make Today A Great Day?

_____

_____

_____

During the evening just before going to bed take a moment
to reflect on your day then List the 3 best things that
happened...

1) _____

_____

_____

2) _____

_____

_____

3) _____

_____

_____

A MESSAGE FROM ME TO YOU

I believe in you…

Remember to be yourself no matter what and to know that you are your biggest fan, always remember that life is a journey of market research and what you choose to do with it is up to you.

When you are in the moment of choosing, always choose good, always be in the choice no matter what, be yourself, love yourself unconditionally, and lastly remember that the choice is truly yours!...
Yasmine Ben Salmi

hebe_boonzaaijer

ABOUT THE AUTHOR

AS HEARD ON RADIO & AS SEEN ON TV & IN NEWSPAPERS & MAGAZINES

Purpose: To eradicate low self-esteem by liberating 1 million young people through the teaching of self love

https://linktr.ee/YasmineBenSalmi

Guest speaker at Equinix "Global Happiness Speaker Series"

Yasmine Ben Salmi aka LovePreneur is an 12yr old award-winning author of a book series called The Choice is Yours; The Choice is Yours - 10 Keys Principles to Create A Happier Lifestyle, The Choice is Yours – Your Thinking C.A.P for Living & Loving Life and The Choice is Yours – When I Chose To Be In The Choice.

Yasmine is a Winner of TruLittle Heros Award - Creative 2017.

Yasmine is a Podcast Host for a show called Life According To Yasmine: https://yasminebensalmi.sounder.fm/show/a-letter-to-your-younger-self

Brunel University London (B.U.L) have given the Ben Salmi family the opportunity to participate in

Masterclasses covering Engineering, Computer Science and currently the Environmental Agency Masterclass.

Yasmine's youngest brother 8-year-old Amire is proud to be the youngest ever honorary STEM Ambassador in history for Brunel University London (B.U.L).

B.U.L has given the homeschooled families the opportunity to participate in masterclasses for the first time in history thanks to Lesley Warren.

Yasmine held her family's signature 2 Day Family workshop called Dreaming Big Together - Mamas Secret Recipe at The Hub Chelsea FC & Virgin Money.

Yasmine and her family have been acknowledged in the credits of a NEW movie called: How Thoughts Become Things movie promotional link:

Bit.ly/HowThoughtsBecomeThingsMovie2020

Yasmine is the founder of The Choice Is Yours Publishing House.

Yasmine hosts her signature program called The Choice Is Yours - Your Thinking C.A.P For Living & Loving Life at Virgin Money Lounge

Yasmine participated in campaigns for Sainsburys, Legoland, Warner Bros, Sony and Made for Mums to name a few.

Yasmine's signature program: Your Thinking C.A.P for Living & Loving Life™

Yasmine is founder of Dog Walking Service "Woof-Woof your dog is here".

Yasmine was nominated for a R.E.E.B.A Award 2017, Winner of Radio Works Authors Awards 2017 and nominated for National Diversity Award 2017.

Yasmine was invited to be a guest speaker at The Beat You Expo: https://youtu.be/Fz9mErJC8rA where there were 15,000 attendees and a former International Radio Show Host

Yasmine is also the founder of Mother and Daughter Connect Collection and founder of Lovepreneur.

Yasmine dreams to be the change that she desires to see in the world and inspire others to be in the choice as often as possible.

The question is when will you start living life on your terms?

Book:

The Choice Is Yours: Your Thinking C.A.P for Living & Loving Life part 2
https://www.amazon.co.uk/dp/1913310167/ref
=cm_sw_r_cp_api_i_yanEEbMNHWH6M

The Choice Is Yours: When I Chose To Be in The Choice
https://www.amazon.co.uk/dp/B08946D6Y9/re
f=cm_sw_r_cp_api_i_GJk1Eb72EDZ5V

My First Day: Transitioning from Girlhood To
Womanhood
https://www.amazon.co.uk/dp/1913310299/ref
=cm_sw_r_em_api_fabc_GGYGMR20HDYS7X
NH2DPB

Facebook page:
Lovepreneure:
https://m.facebook.com/YasmineBenSalmiakaLo
vePrenur/

BEN SALMI FAMILY MANTRA

"BEN SALMI TEAMWORK MAKES THE DREAMWORK

We believe that there is no such thing as failure only feedback.

We also believe that the journey of one thousand miles begins with a single step in the right direction

FAMILY ANTHEM

If you want to be somebody,
If you want to go somewhere,
You better wake up and PAY ATTENTION

I'm ready to be somebody,
I'm ready to go somewhere,
I'm ready to wake up and PAY ATTENTION!

The question is **ARE YOU?**

HOW THOUGHTS BECOME THINGS MOVIE

I

would like to say a huge thanks to Douglas Vermeeren who is the creator of this amazing movie called How Thoughts Become Things and for making these below interviews possible. I am so appreciative to Douglas for including mine and my family's names in the credits of this remarkable movie 🎁 🎥:

CALL TO ACTION:

#1 👀 Watch "How Thoughts Become Things" movie now:

Bit.ly/HowThoughtsBecomeThingsMovie2020

#2 Join our affiliate team to help us spread the word for about How Thoughts Become Things Movie:

Bit.ly/HowThoughtsBecomeThingsAffiliateProgram

HOW THOUGHTS BECOME THINGS

All that a man achieves and all that he fails to achieve is the direct results of his own thoughts.
James Allen

HOW THOUGHTS BECOME THINGS

Dr Travis W Fox

YASMINE BEN SALMI
INTERVIEWING DR TRAVIS W FOX
STAR FROM "HOW THOUGHTS
BECOME THINGS MOVIE"

#1 👀 Watch the full interview on YouTube:
https://youtu.be/5qCpY03tUj4

#2 🎙 Listen to the full interview on my Podcast Show:
https://embed.sounder.fm/e/f6c04216b8c9466f93669a2c12d63
eaf/5LG8z?player_style=blue

YASMINE BEN SALMI
INTERVIEWING MEAGEN FETTES
STAR FROM HOW THOUGHTS
BECOME THINGS MOVIE"

#1 👀 Watch the full interview on YouTube:
https://youtu.be/CQiKi0Zyun8

#2 🎙 Listen to the full interview on my Podcast Show:
https://embed.sounder.fm/e/f6c04216b8c9466f93669a2c12d63
eaf/ALlqz?player_style=blue

HOW THOUGHTS BECOME THINGS

All that a man achieves and all that he fails to achieve is the direct results of his own thoughts.
James Allen

#1 •• Watch the full interview on YouTube:
https://youtu.be/KOoCnU4ffVs

#2 ▪ Listen to the full interview on my Podcast Show:
https://embed.sounder.fm/e/f6c04216b8c9466f93669a2c12d63eaf/0zBg7?player_style=blue

HOW THOUGHTS BECOME THINGS

All that a man achieves and all that he fails to achieve is the direct results of his own thoughts.
James Allen

MARIE DIAMOND

YASMINE BEN SALMI INTERVIEWING MARIE DIAMOND STAR FROM "THE SECRET & HOW THOUGHTS BECOME THINGS MOVIE"

#1 •• Watch the full interview on YouTube:
https://youtu.be/xsMvV_9gsgo

#2 ▪ Listen to the full interview on my Podcast Show:

The Choice Is Yours - I'm Not Just A Pretty F.A.C.E, I AM Intelligent Too

https://embed.sounder.fm/e/f6c04216b8c9466f9366
9a2c12d63eaf/gDmKz?player_style=blue

HOW THOUGHTS BECOME THINGS

All that a man achieves and all that he fails to achieve is the direct results of his own thoughts.
James Allen

HOW THOUGHTS BECOME THINGS

Bob Doyle

YASMINE BEN SALMI INTERVIEWING BOB DOYLE STAR FROM "HOW THOUGHTS BECOME THINGS MOVIE"

#1 👀 Watch the full interview on YouTube:
https://youtu.be/2dkoRlhuayo

#2 🎧 Listen to the full interview on my Podcast Show:
https://embed.sounder.fm/e/f6c04216b8c9466f9366
9a2c12d63eaf/kLNJL?player_style=blue

MICHEL VAN DE LOGT
JAMES DOUGLAS BOND

PAT ALVATER
SOAR TO SUCCESS MAGAZINE

CURTIS G ELLIS
THE EDGE MAGAZINE

SABRINA BEN SALMI
LASHAI BEN SLAMI
TRAY-SEAN BEN SALMI
YASMINE BEN SALMI
PAOLO BEN SALMI
AMIRE BEN SALMI

ADAM COX
RAQUEL DIEHM

ENTREPRENEUR SUCCESS MAGAZINE

ME & MY FAMILY

Me and my siblings have a host of products and services that we have designed to empower you to touch the hearts and minds of others for generations to come. Please do not hesitate to get in touch to plant a seed for your future

Plant a tree in our Ben Salmi forest:
https://forestnation.com/net/forests/bensalmifamilyforest/

The Choice Is Yours - I'm Not Just A Pretty F.A.C.E, I AM Intelligent Too

1 Family   **6 DREAMS**   1 Mission

The Choice Is Yours - I'm Not Just A Pretty F.A.C.E, I AM Intelligent Too